**From the TikTok creator of
"Texts from My College Freshman"
comes a collection celebrating the
humor of the modern teenager.**

When Chip Leighton started sharing the funny,
weird, crazy things his kids said and texted, he
quickly learned he was not alone. Since launching,
his channel has become the go-to support group for
adults with teenagers in their lives. Parents world-
wide use Leighton's posts to laugh, commiserate,
and share their own kids' classics, like "Do I have
Medicare?" and "Where do I buy pasta water?" or
"Don't wear mom jeans to my school again." In this
debut collection, Leighton showcases hundreds of
these gems, plus plenty of tongue-in-cheek advice.

what
time is
noon

what time is noon

Hilarious Texts, Ridiculous
Feedback, and Not-So-Subtle
Advice from Teenagers

CHIP LEIGHTON

Countryman Press

An Imprint of W. W. Norton & Company
Independent Publishers Since 1923

For information about permission to reproduce selections from this
book, write to Permissions, Countryman Press, 500 Fifth Avenue,
New York, NY 10110

For information about special discounts for bulk purchases, please
contact W. W. Norton Special Sales at specialsales@wwnorton.com
or 800-233-4830

Manufacturing by Versa Press
Book design by Allison Chi
Illustrations by Chrissy Kurpeski
Production manager: Devon Zahn

Countryman Press
www.countrymanpress.com

An imprint of W. W. Norton & Company, Inc.
500 Fifth Avenue, New York, NY 10110
www.wwnorton.com

978-1-68268-924-0

10 9 8 7 6 5 4 3 2 1

To Matthew and Laura,
the best (and most sarcastic) kids
any parent could hope for

Contents

Introduction

IMAGINE BEING A teenager and your dad starts going viral on social media with his cringy videos. Now you understand my kids' plight: having the embarrassing dad who, in the words of my daughter, is "craving validation through TikTok." Since you can never have enough validation, I figured I would double down and write a book. And to make it even worse, I'm focusing on teenagers.

Anyone who's been around teenagers knows the funny things they say—and text. It can be hard to keep a straight face when a kid asks, "I'm at the store. Where do I find the pasta water?" Whether you're raising, teaching, coaching, working with, or just randomly interacting with teens, you'll probably recognize many of the quotes in this book. You may even remember some from your own teenage years. And if you're a teenager now (with a great sense of humor, since you're reading this book!), you've probably written a few of these texts recently.

A couple years ago, I started sharing my family's funny quotes and stories online under an account called *The Leighton Show*. Posts like "Texts from My College Freshman" or "Things I've Apologized to My Teenagers For" struck a chord, and my comment sections were flooded with parents telling me they're living the same lives. My account became a kind of support group for parents of teens, with many sharing their own hysterical stories.

What follows is a celebration of teen humor: funny texts and conversations, tongue-in-cheek advice, charts and graphs to spell it all out, and some not-too-serious quizzes to test your knowledge.

I've included the best of the "dumb" questions teens ask, including "Can I use a Christmas stamp to mail something in July?" or "Do I go in where it says entrance?" Most of these questions aren't really stupid; they're just reminders of things we never thought to teach our kids (although the entrance one is a little concerning . . .).

You're also likely familiar with the endless instructions teenagers give their parents about not embarrassing or annoying them. "Don't say my name in public" or "You laugh too much. Especially when you're with your friends" or "Could you breathe any louder?" are a few examples in a very long list that all boil down to staying as invisible as possible, as long as you're still able to finance their DoorDash account.

I've learned a lot of important rules of survival like this

from other parents, but I didn't realize a funny quirk of texts until I wrote this book. You'll see that some texts are capitalized and others are not, which may seem like a publisher error, since phones automatically default to capitalization. Asking my kids revealed that many teenagers deliberately change their phone's settings to eliminate capital letters. I think this is hysterical and one of the most teen things I can think of.

Speaking of survival, I'm including sections throughout the book called "Parent Perspectives." Much like the comment sections on my social media posts (or my direct message inbox), these pages let parents confess to the super-annoying things they do ("Apparently when I'm sitting, I move my feet too much") or recount the brutal feedback their kids have given them ("Your job aged you like the President"). Many of these comments are paraphrased, since I receive so many messages with similar themes (I guess a lot of you move your feet way too much).

You'll also get glimpses into my own family through recurring "Leighton Family Moment" sections. Writing the book has of course led to more feedback from my teens relating to my dubious "influencer" status. When I left my corporate job shortly before starting the book, the thrust of the feedback from my daughter shifted to: "Look, a middle-aged man with no source of income." And, with a more concerned tone, "Do we have to fly Spirit Airlines now?"

While I sprinkle some silly advice throughout the book, my real advice about the teen years is simple: laugh a lot and remember that we were all teenagers once. And, of course, be kind when reminding them that pasta water is made by cooking pasta in water.

Oh, and don't breathe so loud.

I Facetimed my daughter the other day. She answered, looked in the camera and said,

"NO."

A mom who now knows she should stick to texting

CHAPTER 1

Communicating

THESE DAYS, YOU'VE got a lot of options when communicating with teens. Texts, emails, in-person conversations, phone calls, video calls, etc. Unfortunately, none of these will work. I think the root of the problem is that your kids don't want to hear from you. This obviously changes if they need money or a password. Your kids will initiate these conversations, which leads to a good rule of thumb: don't speak unless spoken to.

Group chats might seem like a fun and convenient way to stay connected with your kids. Sadly, your kids may not see it this way. In reviewing our family group chat once, I realized the only messages for the past 30 days were my own, to which no one had responded. The one exception: my daughter used the "thumbs down" on one text, because it indicated what time we were leaving in the morning. I've heard from multiple parents that their kids just removed themselves from the family chat.

If you're desperate, you could always try commenting on their social media pages, but these comments will be deleted immediately without being read.

"the emoji isn't necessary"

And Other Typical Teenager Texts

One great quality of teens is that they cut right to the point.

Brah, pick me up at 3
and don't embarrass me

Stop texting me

do not tag me

Park a block away

stop liking my friends
posts on IG

Choose Your Communication Method Carefully

PROBABILITY OF RESPONSE

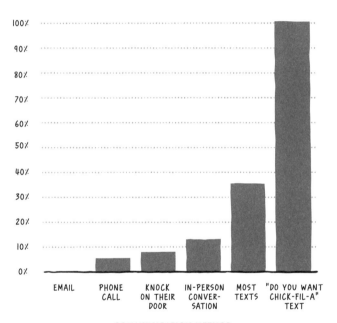

COMMUNICATION METHOD

Top Responses if You Try Actually Calling Your Teenager on the Phone

(Like People Did in the 20th Century)

1. **THEY TEXT YOU WHILE THE PHONE IS RINGING.** Variations of this text include:
   - "what"
   - "why are you calling me?"
   - "stop calling me"
   - "no"
2. **THEY ANSWER AND IMMEDIATELY HANG UP.**
3. **IT RINGS TO VOICEMAIL.** There are two variations to this scenario:
   - "This voicemail box has not been set up."
   - They have recorded a fake voicemail that makes it sound as if they answered: "Hey. Can you hear me? Hello?" You will sound like an idiot trying to speak to them for 30 seconds before you realize what's going on.
4. **THEY PICK UP AND DON'T SAY ANYTHING.** Make sure you listen to hear if the phone has stopped ringing, because otherwise you'll annoy them by making them wait for you to start talking.

"Where's the closest ER? Don't freak"

And Other Texts You Don't Want to Receive from Your Kids

Unfortunately, these are all real.

You might get a letter from Caesars Palace banning me from entering until I'm 21

U-Haul might call you right now.

send me a pic of your signature. Don't ask questions pls

Our starting catcher's roommate does tattoos

My Communication Mistakes, According to My Teens

Telling them things they already know

Usually, when I try to share helpful pieces of information such as, "Your cousins are coming over on Thanksgiving," the response is "Mom already told me that" in an exhausted tone as they leave the dinner table. Sorry that Mom and I aren't telepathic.

Misspeaking

If I mispronounce a word or jumble a sentence, the response is usually, "What's wrong with you??" They often bring up the time I tried unsuccessfully to tell them we were walking through some excellent rabbit habitat. In my defense, try saying those last two words while out of breath on a hike.

Asking too many questions

Are we allowed to go to your track meet? What are you doing this summer? Whose house were you at last night? "Nobody you know" is the standard answer to the last one.

Lack of Context

A teenager's failure to provide context (and their refusal to take follow-up questions) can make you wonder sometimes.

i need to go to the dentist. i chipped my teeth. don't feel like explaining.

Send pictures of pets we used to have. URGENT

I'm in jail . . . . . . I didn't do anything.

Need AAA login, I'm fine just need car towed.

can you bring me my science homework and $300

Pop Quiz: Texting

Which of the following should you NOT use in your text messages?

A. Periods ⟶ "the period came off as very passive aggressive idk if you meant that"

B. More than four words

C. Full sentences

D. Paragraphs

E. Hashtags

F. Emojis

G. The full expression "OK"

H. Questions for them

I. Anything voice-texted

J. Signing off with your name

K. Expressions of emotion

L. All of the above

Answer: Obviously, it's L. The proposed formats are roughly in order of offensiveness. If you use periods, your kid will think you're furious. The list gets worse after that. I know you'll be tempted to use emojis, but don't. I know of an unfortunate mom who used the eggplant emoji to tell her kids what was for dinner.

Are We Speaking the Same Language?

Phrases Your Kids Don't Understand

"**QUARTER TO 10**": They are vaguely aware this originates from some old-fashioned type of clock but don't have the energy to learn the translation. "OMG just say the real time!"

"**YOUR SOCIAL**": When someone at the bank asks your teen for their "social" (security number), the typical response is: "Mostly TikTok, but I've been getting more into Insta lately."

"**DOB**": If they see this on a form, most kids will leave it blank, but some will text you: "do i have a dob?"

"**10-4**": One mom told me her son overslept and called his boss to tell him he'd be late. The boss told him "10-4 good buddy." The kid thought he had new hours.

"**IT'S TIME TO GET UP**": This one never seems to penetrate.

Most Common Texts from My Son

Questions You Should NOT Ask Your Kids

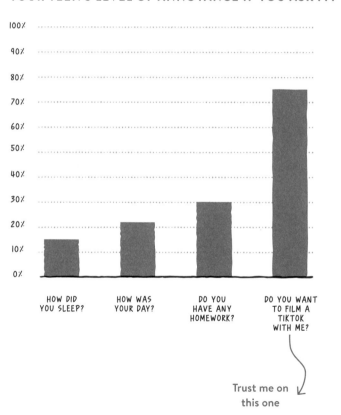

YOUR TEEN'S LEVEL OF ANNOYANCE IF YOU ASK . . .

100%

90%

80%

70%

60%

50%

40%

30%

20%

10%

0%

HOW DID YOU SLEEP?

HOW WAS YOUR DAY?

DO YOU HAVE ANY HOMEWORK?

DO YOU WANT TO FILM A TIKTOK WITH ME?

Trust me on this one

Pop Quiz:
Good Morning!

If you say good morning to your teenager, they will:

A. Quietly mutter, "No, it's not."

B. Hold a hand in the air to indicate "stop."

C. Shout, "Oh my God!"

D. Text you: "why do you have to be like this"

Answer: N/A. Parents of teens know better than to say this.

> "I had morning sickness"
> was the excuse one teenage
> boy gave when he was
> late for school.

Pop Quiz: Is This a Good Time for an In-Person Conversation?

Which of the following excuses does your teen offer? Score a point for each answer that applies.

- I'm about to shower
- I can't deal with this right now
- I have to go to the bathroom
- I'm too tired
- I just started a video game
- I'm about to go out
- I just got home
- I'm going to sleep
- I'm eating
- I'm "studying"
- I can't with you right now
- No response: they immediately disappear into their room

Score of 1 to 3: Your kid is obviously not a teenager. Recheck your answers or their birth certificate.

Score of 4 to 8: Good news. Your teenager is normal. Hopefully you enjoy talking to yourself.

Score of 9 to 12: Good luck. You may need to hire a private detective to find out where they're going to college.

How the Ratios Break Out

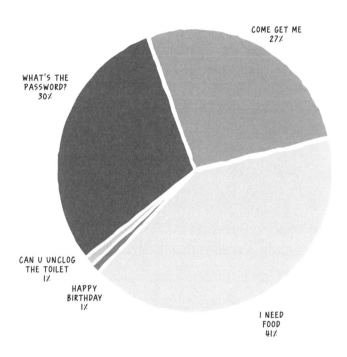

TEXTS FROM YOUR TEEN

COME GET ME
27%

WHAT'S THE
PASSWORD?
30%

CAN U UNCLOG
THE TOILET
1%

HAPPY
BIRTHDAY
1%

I NEED
FOOD
41%

Hopefully the toilet
and birthday texts
come on different days.

Typical Conversations with My Kids

Question: What are you studying in environmental science?
Answer: "The environment."

Question: What did that federal prosecutor talk to you about on career day?
Answer: "Federal prosecuting."

Question: Wasn't that a great vacation we took?
Answer: "OK?"

Question: Where are you working this summer?
Answer: "It's like some office or something."

Question: Who is that friend you were talking to?
Answer: "What do you want, her life story?"

Timing Is Everything

Sometimes the reasonableness of a request can be undermined by its timing, as the examples below demonstrate.

- At 8:00 p.m. on Thursday:

> need a pair of black converses an oversized t-shirt and a quart of chocolate milk by Saturday night

- At 1:00 a.m. from 4 hours away:

> there's a bug in my room

- Two days before prom:

> I need an outfit for prom . . . and one of those flower things you get the girl

- At 12:32 a.m.:

> mom are you up rn I need a verification code

- At any time of day or night, with no advanced notice:

> can u apple pay me i'm next in line at wawa

True Confessions from Parents Who Have Embarrassed Their Teenagers

- I said my daughter's name in a movie theater lobby and she got upset because she knew someone behind the counter.
- When I called the waiter by his name, my kids informed me I wasn't on a first name basis with him.
- I said hello to my daughter's friend in a "voice meant for a toddler."
- My son told me I'm too enthusiastic.
- My daughter accused me of saying "have a nice day" too aggressively to the cashier.
- I'm no longer allowed to say "hi" and ask what floor in an elevator.
- I was accused of using a fake voice at the McDonald's drive-through: "Why do you have to say 'thanks' like that? Just use your normal voice."
- My son told me I pronounce his name wrong.

Word Counts

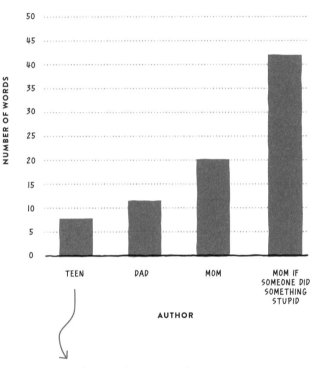

AVERAGE LENGTH OF TEXTS

"Stop texting paragraphs.
I'm not reading all that."

More Typical Teenager Texts

someone just rang the doorbell

turn off your music when you pick me up

You can come in the living room now. We're taking a break.

don't wave at my friends when you pick me up

Why do you keep putting a thumbs up on my messages, it seems so passive aggressive

I'm putting you on silent

Stop trying to make connections with people. It's embarrassing.

"You have to Feed Me. You're Literally My Guardian."

My daughter, 30 minutes after I prepared her last snack

CHAPTER 2

Food

THE COMMENT THAT "we literally have nothing to eat" is a given, especially after I've just unloaded hundreds of dollars of groceries. This is probably because I didn't buy any actual food (like Pop Tarts) but only purchased "ingredients" (like eggs). Kids can be demanding when it comes to food. I was once told that the smoothie I made was too cold. It's ironic because most teenagers lack some very basic knowledge about food. I was stunned one day to learn that my 15-year-old did not know that popcorn comes from corn ("news to me").

My basic advice is that teens will eat anything as long as it comes from Chipotle or Chick-fil-A. Beyond that, you're just rolling the dice. Below are some glimpses into what you can expect when feeding your teen (which, as my daughter often reminds me, you're "technically required" to do).

The Other White Meat

I usually give up red meat for Lent, which really cramps the family's dining style. Last year, I served a slow-cooked pork shoulder to which I had added a little too much liquid smoke. "How is it?" I asked my daughter. "You should have given up liquid smoke for Lent," she replied.

"Peeps cereal. Need it."

And Other Teen Food Quotes

One time our toaster broke and I suggested my daughter could toast her bagel in the oven. Her response: "I'm not doing that. We're not living in the 1800s."

Here are some other gems from your kids:

"I have to eat oatmeal for dinner?!? What is this, the Great Depression?"

"Don't call orange juice 'OJ.' That's weird."

"We need pasta. Preferred shapes: rotini, penne rigate, radiatore, or whatever."

"Can you pass the salad lotion?"

"How much longer are you going to be chewing that apple? Can't you go to the basement or something?"

"Watching you eat that cookie made me lose my appetite."

"Can't you drink your coffee any quieter?"

"What was that one dressing I liked that one time? Was it Caesar or something?"

"Did you see a lot of fields of pasta when you visited Italy?"

"Make sure no one drinks my doctor pepper."

Meal Reviews from My Kids

MEAL	REVIEW
HOMEMADE VEGETABLE SOUP AND BREAD	MEDIEVAL PEASANT FOOD
CHICKEN, EGG NOODLES, AND CARROTS	BASIC
AVOCADO TOAST	THE BREAD TOASTING WAS SUBPAR
ANY SLIGHTLY REVISED RECIPE	WHY ARE WE EXPERIMENTING WITH DINNER?
GRILLED CHEESE SANDWICH	UNEVENLY SLICED
HAM SANDWICH	AVERAGE
CHICKEN TORTILLA SOUP	TOO HOT
STEAK, POTATOES, AND BROCCOLI	CAVE PERSON MEAL

Ways to Embarrass Your Kids: Food Edition

You may think you already understand everything that will annoy your kid. But did you know eating a banana too loud will do the trick? Yup. One mom reported that her "loud chewing" was the source of all her son's stress, anxiety, and failing grades. Here's more:

- At the supermarket, I asked my son if we needed popcorn, and he shushed me because it was "embarrassing to be talking about our food situation in public."
- I asked for ketchup in a restaurant and was told it made me a "Karen."
- I stabbed my salad too aggressively.
- My son informed me I was making way too much noise while drinking water.
- Our waiter forgot to bring tortillas with my fajitas and my teens said I was being rude because I asked the waiter if he could bring them.

Pickles Grow in Swamps

And More *Real Examples* of Teen Misconceptions about Food

- Artichoke hearts come from a pig.
- Zucchini sticks contain fish.
- Steak fries have meat in them.
- Rice is made in a factory.
- Pillsbury crescent rolls roll themselves up in the oven.

> "Did you get the boneless chicken? How do they walk if they don't have bones?"
>
> —17-year-old

"Is dry white wine a powder?"

And Other Relevant Questions

"Is a 13 x 9 pan the same as a 9 x 13 pan?"

"Which one's the stove?"

"What are the peppermint sticks at Christmas called? Shaped like a cane?"

"Are my eggs gonna taste weird if I take them from different cartons?"

"What are the white cubes in fruit cocktail? Potatoes?"

"How does eating cold turkey help you quit smoking?"

"What does 'brown the hamburger' mean?"

"Can I trust a gas station egg?"

"Are parsnips chicken?"

"Do I drink fat-free or skim milk?"

"Does the meat come in the taco kit?"

"What's the wet stuff in soup?"

"Does the cardboard stay on the pizza when I put it in the oven?"

"Where's the silver thing that cooks the eggs?"

"Are scallops meat? I thought they were a type of onion."

"Chicken broth. It's not the sweat of the chicken, is it?"

My Food Mistakes,
According to My Teens

Sometimes my kids aren't too impressed with what I'm eating. "You're literally a grown man eating cookie dough" or "You're drinking a glass of milk like a little baby" are examples of feedback I've received. Most of the critiques, however, relate to what food I bought or didn't buy. I once had to apologize because I couldn't get fried chicken from our favorite restaurant after it went out of business. Some of my other mistakes include:

- I bought the "old-fashioned" kind of cheese that isn't presliced.
- Cooking the steak in the air fryer was "a miss."
- I chose the "BS whole grain waffles."
- The bananas I bought were too curved.

I once sent my daughter a funny video of a panda chewing on bamboo.

"You eating food," was her reply.

Food Storage and Safety

This is not the strong suit of many kids. One girl in college asked her mom if she could eat her leftover chicken alfredo for breakfast. She didn't have a fridge, but she had set it in front of the fan overnight. Some other classics:

"Mom, I left a hot dog on the mantel, can you please put it in the fridge?"

"I put my salad in the freezer for later."

"The white fuzzy stuff growing on my strawberries is fine to eat, right?"

List of Actual Foods Found in Teenagers' Bedrooms
- Half a pizza under the bed that he was "saving for later but forgot about"
- Burrito bowl shoved between the bed and the wall
- Olive Garden blackened chicken pasta stored under the bed for a week
- Five-month-old hard-boiled egg that had fallen between the bed frame

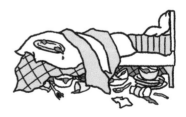

The State of the Kitchen

Some things you might notice in a teen-used kitchen . . .

YOU'LL NEED TO STIR YOUR COFFEE WITH A KNIFE.
Spoons (or forks, for that matter) are nowhere to be found.
Actually, you might find them but not in the kitchen. Try
under the bed, in the yard, or in the trash (or possibly at
school).

MOST PACKAGES IN THE PANTRY WILL BE EMPTY.
Some will contain traces of food but will almost certainly
be unsealed. I've had mothers tell me that teaching their
teenagers to open and close a box of cereal was harder than
giving birth to them.

**THE KITCHEN WILL BE ARTFULLY DECORATED WITH
RAMEN SHARDS.** You will find them on the stovetop
and muffin crumbs on every surface. Fourteen dirty water
glasses and an empty paper towel roll will complement
these nicely.

**A MILK JUG CONTAINING 3 DROPS OF MILK WILL
BE IN THE FRIDGE.** It could be worse: a mom sent me a
picture of her pantry one morning with a full gallon of milk
on the shelf next to the cereal. Wild night, I guess.

"Low key, it was mid."
And Other Teen Food Reviews

"We don't like when you marinate stuff."

"You've cooked better."

On being served spaghetti: "Why didn't you make linguine?"

"I don't like cream cheese from our house."

When served roast beef with veggies, salad, and mashed potatoes: "Can you make a really nice dinner tomorrow?"

"Can you tell me how to make chicken breasts but not dry like you make them?"

"Did dad seriously just offer my friend pork schnitzel for dinner?"

Teen Food Knowledge

I've heard multiple stories of kids who wanted half a sandwich, so they pulled out two slices of bread, cut each in half, and put the unused halves back in the bag. Here are some other classics that parents have shared with me:

- My son asked how to make ice. He didn't know if "anything special needed to be added."
- When I found my daughter mixing the brownie batter with her hand, she said, "What? The box says mix by hand."
- My daughter ordered a popcorn chicken salad without the popcorn.
- My daughter thought ham was its own animal.
- When I ordered a pizza half-cheese and half-pepperoni, the teenager on the phone asked which half I wanted the pepperoni on.
- My son flipped the baking pan over and told me, "It says grease and flour the bottom of the pan."
- My daughter told me excitedly, "Mom, I had placenta for dinner last night."

Deliver Me

It used to be that when parents had a date night, they could just leave behind a frozen pizza for the kids. Not anymore. "It's fine, we'll just order something and charge it to your credit card." This ends up costing more than mom and dad's meal out. And that's just one of today's new delivery occasions. Eventually it won't faze you when your child quietly retrieves a Wingstop bag from the front porch at 10:30 p.m.

When the doorbell rings during dinner, it's not a good sign. Examples of deliveries you might expect during dinner:

- 10-piece Chicken McNuggets
- Taco Bell Chalupa combo box
- Pint of gelato, perfectly timed for dessert (though you will not be offered any)

> "Can you DoorDash me some DQ to the park where I'm at on my field trip?"

I took my son and his friend to IHOP. He asked me to sit at a different table . . . by myself.

The mom of a teenager
(aka just the Uber driver)

Pop Quiz: How Ready Are Your Kids for Dinner?

What do your kids do when you tell them dinner will be ready in 5 minutes? Score a point for every "yes" answer.

- Start a new video game that will take 45 minutes
- Open a 12 oz. bag of Doritos
- Pop four Eggo waffles in the toaster
- Say: "I'm not really hungry, I just ate lunch."
- Make a smoothie
- Disappear into the bathroom for 30 minutes
- Whip up a quick batch of ramen
- Order DoorDash

Scoring: Anything less than 5 is pretty good, honestly. If you're 5 or over, just accept the reality that your kid will likely be crushing a Popeye's chicken sandwich while you're pulling the steaks off the grill.

Note: If this list was about me,
it would need to include starting
a random house project.

Don't Forget to Tip Your Server

For the level of service kids demand, we really should be getting tipped.

"Reheat my lasagna and make sure there are no cold spots."

"Make me pancakes. Do it."

"Don't call me down to dinner until the food has been plated."

"Make me breakfast. And not that stupid frittata thing."

"More cornbread. Stat."

I'm literally standing outside. Literally arrive.

My daughter, when I was 1 minute late
after swim practice ended 5 minutes early

CHAPTER 3

In the Car

THERE ARE TWO main problems with the car. First, the car forces your kid to be within several feet of you for a prolonged period. This puts them on the defensive because they fear you may try to speak to them or play your music.

The second problem is that your teenager will eventually be driving this vehicle. The terror your teen feels when you blast Wham! on the radio will pale in comparison with your experience as their passenger. Handle gripping, phantom braking, and cold sweats are all perfectly normal. I'm pretty sure the driving exam is the one test you hope your kid will fail.

"I don't even know how an intersection works."

And Other Actual Quotes from Kids Learning to Drive

After one session of Drivers' Ed, your teen will suddenly be an expert at driving and will criticize your every move. It's ironic because the same child who questions whether you came to a full stop will soon be barreling through the same intersection after they "zoned out for a minute."

"Mom, I don't know why you're so mad. The lady I hit wasn't even this mad."

After not waiting his turn at a 4-way stop: "I was establishing my dominance."

"I thought as long as I didn't hit the kid it was legal."

"I could drive fine if the instructor would stop grabbing the wheel."

"They told us in Drivers' Ed if you drink and drive, they'll give you a UTI."

"Will I get in trouble for driving with roller skates on?"

"When they say 10 o'clock and 2 o'clock, how do I know where the clock is?"

"I think I hit a pheasant, not the person, the bird."

"Where am I? I don't remember the last few turns I took."

"This is just like a video game."

"How do I turn on night mode?"

"So, when you do a hit and run . . . how does that work?"

"I don't use my mirrors because I can hear when a car is coming."

"Can you scroll up the window?"

"Stop screaming every time we almost crash."

"Which side is the gas hole on?"

"I'm really good at blinkers."

After causing a man to jump off the side of the road and dive into the bushes: "So dramatic."

"I don't like driving at night. I can't see the pedals."

"I feel like I'm about to lose control of the car."

"Relax, bruh. I've got my license now."

One mom told me her daughter hit a parked car at the exact moment she was telling a kid in the back seat what a good driver she was. Below are some other things you should fear:

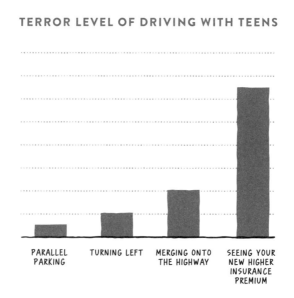

TERROR LEVEL OF DRIVING WITH TEENS

PARALLEL PARKING · TURNING LEFT · MERGING ONTO THE HIGHWAY · SEEING YOUR NEW HIGHER INSURANCE PREMIUM

> Dad, I want you to teach me to drive. Mom yells at everything I do. You just yell when I put us in danger.

Ways I've Embarrassed Myself in the Car

I panicked in a parking lot.

Once, while parked at a rest stop, the car next to us backed up and I freaked out because I thought our car was rolling forward. I started slamming on the brakes, grabbing the wheel, and looking ridiculous. This happened 4 years ago, and my teens remind me of it every time I park the car.

When I shared this online, I realized it happens to other people, too. One guy who was parked in his driveway when the garage door started going up thought his car was sinking into the ground.

I was startled by sound of a car horn.

This turned out to be a false alarm: it was just the radio. According to my daughter, I should have been able to figure this out from context clues. If you're not familiar with the idea of context clues, it basically means you're an idiot if you can't connect the dots (the key dot here was the lyric "beep beep is that my bestie in a Tessie?")

I accidentally drove our car onto a ferry.

This was in Quebec, and the guy who I thought was a parking lot attendant was talking really fast in French and making a lot of confusing hand gestures. Keep in mind I took Spanish in high school.

> "Can you lay the passenger seat all the way back?
> You're embarrassing me sitting there."

What to Expect on Long-Distance Car Trips

- **Incommunicado:** Headphones or earbuds will end all ability to communicate with your teenager for the duration of the trip. Try texting them (for their food order) if you're the passenger.
- **Turn down your "music":** You'll be instructed not to play your horrible music. I guess it will seep in through their headphones, unlike anything you say to them.
- **Behind the wheel:** Most families limit learner's permit driving to local outings. But if you put your teen behind the wheel for a road trip, you can expect numerous terror-filled highway merges.
- **Leg room:** Because teenagers are bigger, they need more leg room. Instead of adjusting your seat a safe and comfortable distance from the wheel, you'll need to cram it forward.
- **Food:** You have absolutely no chance of finding a restaurant everyone agrees on. The "I'm hungry" complaints will start 10 minutes into the trip and won't stop at any time before you arrive (or after).

When one teen's mom opened a bag of chips in the car: "Hold on. I need to put in my ear buds before you start in on that."

Dashboard Warning Lights

Teenagers rarely interpret these correctly and usually refer to them as "emojis." For reference, here is a rundown of the most common ones:

ICON	MEANING	TEENAGER INTERPRETATION
	OIL LOW	TEA KETTLE *ALSO: GENIE LAMP OR GRAVY BOAT* MEANING: THEY HAVE NO IDEA.
	HIGH BEAMS	JELLYFISH *ALSO: SHOWERHEAD* MEANING: WET ROAD?
	FUEL LEVEL	BATTERY? "THE SCREEN SAYS I'M AT TWO BARS."
	AIR-CONDITIONING	SNOWFLAKE. "I THINK IT HELPS YOU DRIVE IN THE WINTER."

How Spending Will Change
with a New Driver

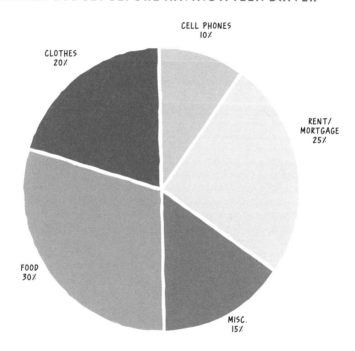

FAMILY BUDGET BEFORE HAVING A TEEN DRIVER

CELL PHONES
10%

CLOTHES
20%

RENT/
MORTGAGE
25%

FOOD
30%

MISC.
15%

FAMILY BUDGET WITH A TEEN DRIVER

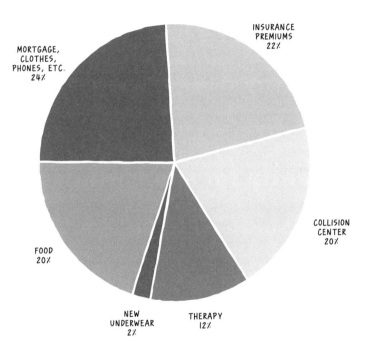

INSURANCE
PREMIUMS
22%

MORTGAGE,
CLOTHES,
PHONES, ETC.
24%

COLLISION
CENTER
20%

FOOD
20%

NEW
UNDERWEAR
2%

THERAPY
12%

During the vision test for her driver's license, they told my daughter to read line five. After sitting silently for a long while she said, "Oh, out loud?"

A mom who now rides in the passenger seat in a constant state of panic

Teen Car "Knowledge"

I guess we all had to learn this stuff at some point, right?

"Which pedal is for reverse?"

"My friend helped me replace the brakes on my car. We didn't replace the back ones because I don't back up that often."

When given a digital tire gauge for Christmas: "Do I just stick it against the side of the tire?"

Standing in front of the car with the hood up: "Where does the gas go?"

"What does the 'No Outlet' sign mean? You can't charge your phone?"

When AAA asked her for license plate number: "The one on the front or the one on the back?"

"The windshield replacement place closes in 2 minutes. Do they finish or do I drive without it?"

"Can I leave a parking space if the meter hasn't run out yet?"

Vroom Vroom!

My Teens' Complaints about My Driving

- **I took half a second to unlock the car doors.** I believe the handle was jiggled 40 times during this span.
- **My arrival estimate for an 8-hour car trip was 5 minutes off.** Teens expect the level of precision NASA employs in calculating the orbit of satellites. It's ironic because when they say they'll be out of the bathroom in 5 minutes, it means 30.
- **I glanced in the side mirror and my daughter thought I was looking at her.** "What are you staring at??" Just that 18-wheeler, sorry.

> Whatever you do, don't put your blinker on one second too early as this will embarrass your teen. It's weird and nobody does that.

Not So Fast

Insurance companies know what they're doing when they set the rates.

TEEN DRIVER'S AVERAGE SPEED

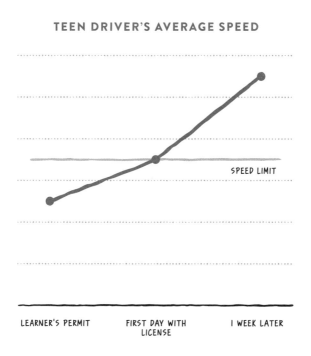

SPEED LIMIT

LEARNER'S PERMIT — FIRST DAY WITH LICENSE — 1 WEEK LATER

Quiz: Teen Driving

Can you identify the most common teenager reactions to these driving situations?

When driving with your teen, if you indicate you like the song they're playing, they will:

A. Turn it up so you can hear it better

B. Groan and roll their eyes

C. Immediately turn it off and remove it from their playlist

Answer: C (sometimes accompanied by B)

When a teen is buying gas and the pump asks for their zip code, they will:

A. Enter their zip code from memory

B. Text you, "what's my zip thing. rn"

C. Ask the person next to them what zip code this gas station is in

Answer: Usually B, but I can assure you I didn't make up answer C.

When getting an oil change and the mechanic asks if they want the tires rotated, they will:

A. Check the owner's manual for guidance
B. Hesitantly mutter, "Um . . . sure"
C. Say, "No thanks, I drive a lot so they're pretty rotated."

Answer: Either B or C, but sometimes they'll text you saying they think the guy is trying to pull some scam. When explaining tire rotation to your teen, just say it's when they "switch them around."

If a teen has to park directly next to another car, they will:

A. Slowly and carefully pull into the spot
B. Keep circling to see if another space opens up
C. Turn around and go home

Answer: Usually B, but C is a close second.

Organ Donor Confusion

Kids have no idea what it means when they're asked if they want to be an organ donor when they get their license. The DMV really needs to explain this better. I know of several teens who said no because they thought it meant the authorities could come take an organ whenever they wanted.

Here are some other top responses:

"You mean right now?"

"No. I hate needles."

"Don't I need those to live?"

"Will I get paid?"

"Wait, is it after you die?"

"Can I still have a funeral?"

After looking at driver's license: "What organs did I donate?"

"I thought it was ok to go left on red."

And More Teen Driving Quotes

Whenever you start to question your teen's driving skills, just think of the girl who asked when she could learn how to steer with her knees like her sister does.

"What blinker do I use to go straight?"

"I have my license. Stop holding on like you're gonna die."

"Is my foot on the gas or the brake right now?"

"Do the odometer numbers go up or down?"

"Who knew the gas pump automatically unclips when you drive off with it in your tank?"

"Do I need this weird tire in my trunk?" Then a minute later: "HELLO?!!!! Do I need this weird tire or not?!"

"I think I'm out of windshield sauce."

"Can you go through a drive-thru in the rain?"

"What vintage of gas should I put in?"

"Calm down. I've only had two accidents."

"If I accidentally hit the accelerator at a red light, should I just keep going and commit?" ⟶

When I posted this online the number of people who thought this was a legitimate question was concerning.

"My friends are almost here—make sure Dad stays in the basement."

CHAPTER 4

At Home

MANY TEENS AND parents get along at home. This is probably because they are only together for about 4 hours when you take sleeping into account. The other 20 hours are spent making noise while the other sleeps. Even so, there are plenty of mistakes to be made. "Interrogating" your kids about their day is probably the biggest. Another mistake is being around when their friends come over. It doesn't matter that your name is on the mortgage, kids expect you to disappear in those situations.

Another thing to prepare yourself for is the astounding impact a teenager has on the overall cleanliness of the house—not to mention their impact on your electric bill, since kids don't learn to turn out lights until they get their first apartment (and its accompanying utility bill).

"You do laundry too often. I can't keep up with putting it away."

And Other Teenager Quotes Around the House

"I'm swooping by the house with a friend, could you clean it please?"

"Can you stop moving my stuff in the shower around?"

"Please don't vacuum when I'm sleeping."

Seeing his mom clean the kitchen: "Mom! It's Mother's Day! You can clean the kitchen tomorrow!"

The Night Shift

One time I received feedback that I made too much noise at 11:00 a.m., disrupting my kid's sleep. I was making coffee, having been awakened at 1:00 a.m. by the sound of nachos being microwaved.

When I'm up early, I tiptoe around as quietly as I can. My son takes a slightly different approach. While preparing food in the overnight hours, he slams every cupboard open and shut, flings drawers open at high speeds, and makes other noises that sound as if all our dishware is shattering. This happens between sessions of scream-shouting at his friends while playing multihour video games.

THE NIGHT SHIFT DECIBEL METER

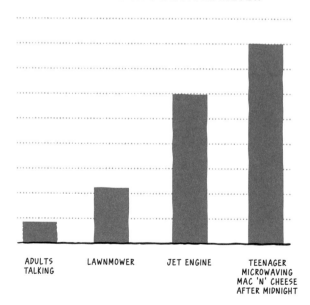

ADULTS TALKING · LAWNMOWER · JET ENGINE · TEENAGER MICROWAVING MAC 'N' CHEESE AFTER MIDNIGHT

Quiz: How to Wake Up a Teen

What time should you wake your teenager up?

A. A few minutes earlier than they asked, so they're not rushed.

B. A few minutes later than they asked, so they can get more rest.

C. At the precise time requested, down to the millisecond, if you know what's good for you.

Answer: None of the above. Your child will be furious, regardless of what time you choose.

What's the best technique for waking a sleeping teen?

A. Enter the room and gently place your hand on their ankle.

B. Whisper in a soft voice, "It's time to get up for school, honey."

C. Stay in the hallway, maintaining a safe distance, and continuously pound on the door while screaming "GET UP" until you hear them growl.

Answer: Definitely C if you value your personal safety.

If your teenager says, "OK, I'm up. Get out!" you should:

A. Leave and don't come back
B. Ask them to speak more politely next time
C. Return in 9 minutes, when you will find them sound asleep again

Answer: C (the human snooze alarm option). Otherwise, you'll hear, "Why did you only wake me up once?? Now I'm late!!"

> After I tried to wake my son no fewer than 10 times for football, he said, "Bro, stop pressing me!" and then "Thanks, Mom, now I'm gonna be late."

Pop Quiz: Is Your Teen Home?

Which of the following indicates that your teenager is home?

A. Their homework and other random things are spread out everywhere

B. The shower has been running for 35 minutes

C. Their bedroom door is closed

D. All the lights are on

E. All of the above

Answer: B. This is a trick question. If you answered E, you forgot that A, C, and D will be true whether your teenager is home or not. Note: If you have a shower speaker, the shower won't end until the Taylor Swift album does.

Ways I've Annoyed My Teens around the House

- **I sneezed more than once:** Typically, my daughter will shout my running sneeze count as it's happening. Once, after *she* sneezed, she turned to me and said, "See how I only sneezed once?"
- **I bought the nonfoaming type of hand soap:** I guess the 3 seconds of lathering is just too much for them.
- **I fast-forwarded 1 second too far:** Sorry that my remote only jumps in 5-second increments. I'm pretty sure we'll still get the gist of what's happening at tribal council.
- **I cleared my throat:** I'm not allowed to do this in my children's presence.
- **I was sitting on the sofa minding my own business:** Sometimes, just existing is all it takes to get the head shake or eye roll.

Quiz: Keeping Things Clean

Let's see how your kid ranks ...

What will your teen do with a dirty cereal bowl?

A. Place in dishwasher
B. Leave it wherever they were eating
C. Slide it under the sofa

After showering, their wet towel goes:

A. On a rack to dry
B. Crumpled on the bathroom floor
C. Thrown in the closet where it will remain hidden for multiple weeks

What items do you regularly find on or near your living room couch?

A. A few partially filled water glasses
B. An open bag of chips, half-spilled
C. Crumpled, dirty socks

If their hands are wet and the paper towel roll is empty,
they will:

A. Relace the roll with a new one
B. Wipe their hands on the empty cardboard insert
C. Wipe their hands on a decorative pillow once they get back to the living room

Mostly As: Congrats. You are raising a future HGTV host.

Mostly Bs: Typical kid. Just chill and stop hassling them.

Mostly Cs: Avoid eye contact when you meet their future roommates and spouses.

> "Mom hasn't stopped rage vacuuming since you left."

We have the exact same personality and laugh all the time, but when I laugh too loud it's over for the night. I get the disgusted look and a door slam.

A mom with a not-so-infectious laugh

"Where is the tool to take my temperature?"

And More Teen Quotes from around the House

Sometimes you hear things around the house that make you realize you need to explain a few things better.

"I think the refrigerator might be broken. The light won't turn on."

"Why are the birds barking so loudly?"

When asked to help vacuum: "Do I just plug it in and push it around the room?"

"Hey, Siri, what country speaks Pig Latin?"

"My shower ran out of hot water, so I'm going to use yours."

"For the washing machine: first I turn the knob to the right and then I pour in the 2 sauces?"

Niceness Levels at Home

OCCASIONS WHEN THE FAMILY IS REALLY NICE TO ME

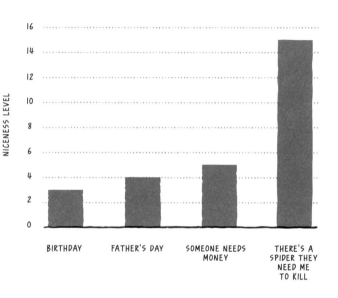

Things That Are Apparently My Fault at Home

- **The smoke alarm was beeping:** I guess I'm supposed to know which smoke alarm it is. Sorry I wasn't born with a bat's echolocation ability. There's nothing I enjoy more than standing in the hallway for 10 minutes, staring at the ceiling looking like an idiot.
- **The dishwasher didn't get everything clean:** When a weird crust was discovered on one of the knives I set on the table, it was assumed to be a "loading issue" caused by me.
- **The Halloween decorations blew around in the wind:** Sorry that I didn't adequately anchor the featherweight foam gravestones to withstand a 40-mph wind.
- **Someone finished the Oreos:** Everyone immediately assumed it was me, but they couldn't prove anything.
- **We lost power:** As a kid, I remember power outages being kind of fun, family board games by candlelight or whatever. For teenagers today, they trigger panic and throw the house into a state of unrest. "Who has a charging brick? Who has a charging brick!!????" "Does the Wi-Fi still work?? Someone answer me!!"

"My kid's friend asked to spend the night. He said it was really bad at their house: the Wi-Fi went out."

Pop Quiz: Phone Chargers

If your teenager has taken your charger and you ask for it back, the response will be:

A. "Nope."

B. "What percent are you at?"

C. "I'm literally at 6%."

D. All of the above

Answer: D. Statements will be made in the following order: B, A, C. If your phone happens to be under 6%, they will just grab the charger and go to their room without responding.

Happy Mother's Day . . .
did you move my charger?

Get Lost

You might think your home is a sanctuary where you can relax. Think again.

"My boyfriend's coming over, can you go in your room and close the door?"

"Dad, please wear socks when my friends come over, you have dry feet."

"You can sit in here, but don't talk to me."

"I'm having a party, can you leave? Go to a hotel or something."

"My friend Jay is coming over. Can you make dad not talk?"

On seeing his mom outside gardening: "Can you go inside? My friend is picking me up."

Out and About

To wrap up this chapter about home, I thought I'd share reminders from other parents that the embarrassment your kids feel at home gets much worse as soon as you leave the house. I'll obviously go much deeper into this theme in the next chapter on high school.

- I wanted to see *Oppenheimer* while my daughter was seeing *Barbie* with a friend. She made me drop her off and go to a different cineplex.
- I bought an orchid yesterday and my son left the store. It was too much for him to see.
- My son got mad because I walked into a Payless Shoes at the mall while he was talking to a girl he knew.
- I once fell on a sidewalk and was pretty banged up. I had to apologize to my daughter for embarrassing her.
- I was waiting for our food at Sheetz. I was just standing there. One kid says, "You're so embarrassing right now," and the other agrees. I hadn't spoken. Nothing.

you can pick me up now just park where no one can see you

CHAPTER 5

High School

IF YOU PLAN to enter school grounds, you should use the teenage guiding principle: "Don't act weird." Unfortunately, even your most basic actions will be seen as weird: walking, talking, waving, clapping, cheering, making eye contact with others, or standing still risk looking stupid. One teen's advice, "Don't ever come into the school to get me—I'll always come out," makes a lot of sense if you think about it.

Assuming you steer clear of school, you'll mainly hear information secondhand through your teen, and some context will be missing. You'll get used to it. Eventually texts like "I need to make 30 things of Canadian bacon tonight" will sound perfectly normal and you won't bother with follow-up questions.

The texts you need to be more concerned about are the ones that start "If the school calls . . . ." These are typically followed by instructions to say you signed a form they forged, or that you should corroborate an outlandish story about an absence.

Ways You've Embarrassed Your Kids at School

Make sure to avoid these egregious mistakes:

- I took notes at a college counselor meeting and wrote too loudly.
- I had to apologize for driving by the high school with bad posture. It wasn't even me.
- My kid told me I walked too loud at her school today.
- I made the mistake of clapping while sitting in an audience with other people clapping.

School Drop-Off and Pickup Etiquette

Once I spaced out and (out of habit) almost dropped my high school freshman daughter off at the middle school. "Why are you like this?" was her response. I guess this is still better than the mom who said she's sent her kids to school several times when it was closed for random holidays she didn't know about.

I know of one dad who fell asleep in the pickup line. No one woke him; they all just went around him. This helps explain texts like, "Please don't send dad. I'm too tired to be embarrassed." Assuming you get to the right school and it's open, try to avoid all the behaviors on the chart opposite. Otherwise, just relax and enjoy this quality time with your child.

> If you live more than 5 minutes away, you should constantly circle the school grounds to prepare for the "we got out early get here now" text.

HOW ANNOYED WILL YOUR TEEN BE IF YOU . . .

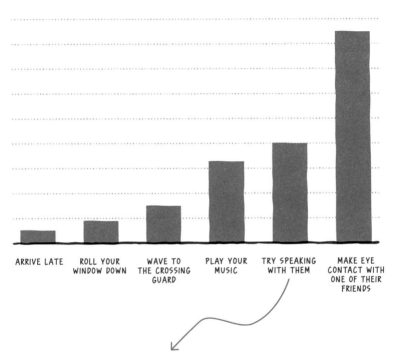

ARRIVE LATE · ROLL YOUR WINDOW DOWN · WAVE TO THE CROSSING GUARD · PLAY YOUR MUSIC · TRY SPEAKING WITH THEM · MAKE EYE CONTACT WITH ONE OF THEIR FRIENDS

When I picked up my daughter
and asked about her day, she replied,
"See, I knew you'd do this."

"I need some plutonium jelly for my science project"

And Other Teenager Texts from School

> Can you send me the pics you took before prom—except not the ones with you and dad in them

> my grade isn't that bad its like a high f

> If we lost the revolutionary war, would we have british accents?

> This physics teacher is unhinged

> hurt my arm a bit may be fractured probably not feeling fine but just going to be chilling the rest of the day

> BTW I have a C in math

Embarrassing Your Kids at Sporting Events

One mother told me she mortified her kid by yelling, "Do not go gently!" during a hockey game. I think I have to side with the kid on that one. I gave my daughter a thumbs-up at a swim meet once, which apparently was embarrassing. I guess thumb gestures are now on the list of prohibited sporting event behaviors, alongside clapping, cheering, or any other detectable expressions of support. Some more examples include:

- My daughter said I shouldn't cheer in full sentences. You're only supposed to cheer in phrases.
- Once, while I was watching a soccer game, my son asked me to stand farther away from the field.
- My son told me my cheering was "too zesty."
- My daughter texted me on the sidelines to ask me to never wear wired headphones to her practice again.
- I was told I was yelling inappropriately at a soccer game, so I said nothing next time and was told that I "wasn't even watching and didn't care."
- While my son was at bat in his baseball game: "I do not need to hear your voice."

Positive ID

Another way to embarrass yourself or your kid is to cheer for the wrong child at a sporting event. These incidents typically involve a dad recording a swimmer finishing in second place while his daughter waits at the wall, having won the race seconds ago. The examples are endless: recording the wrong blonde girl at the ballet recital, the wrong boy receiving his diploma, etc. My favorite is the dad who arrived at a soccer tournament, only to watch the wrong game the entire time. Meanwhile, his daughter was injured on another field and some random dad had to take care of her.

"Is the homecoming game home or away?"

And Other Classic Quotes from High Schoolers

"How come you never taught me that Martha's Vineyard isn't named after Martha Stewart?"

"The Da Vinci Code is how they organize books in a library, right?"

When asked what color his eyes were: "Hazelnut."

"Ash Wednesday's coming up this weekend."

"So, who actually writes my varsity letter?"

"It's pretty weird that they have a nursery inside a Home Depot."

"I tried a cologne at the store I want for Christmas. The brand is called tester."

When learning about the Sistine Chapel: "What happened to the other 15?"

"So how does this whole nine lives thing work?"

"If the school nurse calls, just go with my story."

"I'm thinking of taking a leap year between high school and college."

Historical Confusion

Some teens aren't superclear on all the details about historical figures. Exhibit A:

Son: Do you think Hellen Keller was real?

Mom: What? Of course she was real.

Son: How can you be blind and deaf and fly a plane?
No way.

Mom: She didn't fly a plane.

Son: Yes, she did.

Mom: You're thinking of Amelia Earhart.

Son: Oh, OK.

Things Your Kids Don't Want You Doing

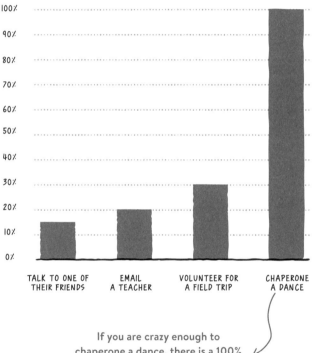

HOW HORRIFIED YOUR TEEN WILL BE IF YOU . . .

If you are crazy enough to chaperone a dance, there is a 100% chance your child will not attend.

"Do we have a zip code?"

And Other Basic Questions

A surprising number of kids think Alaska and Hawaii are located next to each other because they're depicted that way on the map.

"Is a pep talk and a eulogy the same thing?"

"How do you spell LED lights?"

"Do they speak English in London?"

"Where do I get one of those flower croissants for prom?"

"Is a bunny the same thing as a rabbit?"

"How many quarters is football? 3?"

"Do we have any extra vanilla folders?"

"Is my record of birth like real vinyl?"

Upon receiving a letter written in cursive: "Why is this written in Spanish?"

"Do we have insurance on the Keurig?"

Son, after his mom told him he was being annoying: "The feeling is neutral."

"Is my license an ID?"

"Can people survive with only one liver?"

"What time zone are we in? Canada time, right?"

After 3 years of high school Spanish: "When is Cinco de Mayo?"

"What's the name of our mouth doctor?"

"Do I pick you up at arrivals or departures?"

"What time does the ball usually drop on New Year's Eve?"

"Where do wild dogs get their nails clipped?"

"When I turn 18, does that mean I'm not a teenager anymore?"

"What's the difference between gonorrhea and diarrhea?"

what's my shoe size?

CHAPTER 6

College

A LOT OF people know me as the "texts from your college freshman guy," so there is plenty to cover in this chapter. If your kid goes to college, you should expect some interesting texts. Questions like "How do I get my clothes out of the washing machine? Do I just reach in there with my hands?" reflect more on us than them.

Along with laundry, you'll probably discover there are some other adulting skills you neglected to teach them. So don't be fazed when they ask things like, "Does the post office sell stamps?" Hopefully these examples will serve as a reminder of a few things you might want to cover with them now.

The college application process will also provide plenty of classic teen moments. College tours, for example, provide the perfect chance to embarrass your kids with outrageous acts like introducing yourself to other parents ("OMG Stop! No one does that"). Tours also offer insight into your child's priorities. While you may be focused on class size and graduation rates, your kid will be looking to see if there is a Panda Express or Shake Shack in the student center.

"Does the cafeteria deliver?"

And Other Texts from College Freshmen

are we italian?

Do I need a passport to go from Missouri to Arkansas for a football game?

[on the last day of the semester]
How do I wash my sheets?

why didn't you get me the shingles vaccine

[from a college freshman boy]
What's my maiden name?

Am I bilingual?

how tall am I

How do I take the plastic off this Tide Pod?

Are your fingerprints the same on all your fingers?

Do I just open the
tea bag and pour
the tea in the cup?

can you make me an appointment
at the dry cleaners

I'm staying with my friend from September 30-32nd ok?

Did you know George Foreman was a boxer.
I thought he was strictly a grill guy.

can I use my toilet brush
to clean the shower

stop sending toothpaste.
my dorm room is very small

Did I already get my rabies shot?

Did the guinea pig see his shadow

Applying to College Can Be Scary

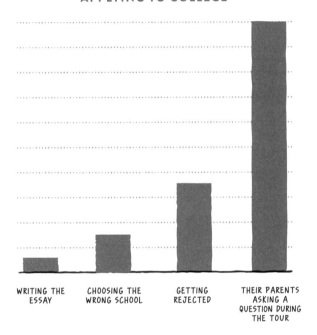

WHAT KIDS FEAR MOST ABOUT APPLYING TO COLLEGE

WRITING THE ESSAY | CHOOSING THE WRONG SCHOOL | GETTING REJECTED | THEIR PARENTS ASKING A QUESTION DURING THE TOUR

Things Your College-Aged Kids Might Be Confused About

Try to keep a straight face when your kids share this stuff:

- My daughter thought the Brita pitcher refilled itself with humidity from the fridge.
- My 18-year-old thought "flamboyant" meant something that can float in water.
- My son thought fresh towels would be delivered to his dorm room daily.
- My college-aged niece thought that time zones changed gradually as you travel (not in hourly increments).
- When my college freshman went looking for the library, she followed the sign that said "bookkeeping." She thought that might be it.

Transcript of Conversation with My Son about His Future College Roommate

Me: Any luck finding a roommate?

Son: Yeah, I told you I found one like 3 weeks ago.

Me: OK—I feel like I would have remembered that, but whatever. What's his name?

Son: Um . . . I don't remember. I can look it up.

Me: Where's he from?

Son: I want to say Maryland or something. Maybe Oregon.

Me: What kind of stuff is he into?

Son: Not sure.

Me: Do you remember literally anything about him?

End of conversation

Ninety seconds later, based only on the information above, my wife successfully located the kid's Instagram account. In his profile picture, he's clearly wearing a fencing uniform. So, unless he's a beekeeper, we now know one thing about him.

How to Embarrass Your Kids During College Visits

Your kids need you to take them on college visits, but they'd prefer you disappear once you arrive on campus. Here are some serious mistakes a few of you have made:

- My daughter said my feet were slapping too loud on the pavement while walking around campus.
- Suggestion from my son on a college visit (family of four): "How about we split into four separate groups?"
- I took a map, when it was offered, at freshman orientation.
- My son asked why I followed so closely behind the tour guide.
- When they opened up a Q&A, my son leaned in and said, "Don't be that mom."

The Most Random Text from College

I adopted a donkey in your name

Fake IDs

I can't prove this, but I think fake IDs are more common than when I was in college. I remember there was one kid who lived down the hall who had one and was super popular as a result. Today, it seems as if every college kid has at least one fake ID and they talk openly about it with their parents. My favorite story is the teen who told his parents he did the math wrong when ordering his ID, so he had to wait 2 more months to use it.

When you walk in the kitchen and your child is photographing their friend against a plain white wall, it's probably not for the yearbook. And if you're in the airport security line and your teen appears to be shuffling through multiple options in their wallet, just hope they pick the right one.

"Can you Venmo this guy $80 for my fake ID?"

"Mom, watch the mail. There are 26 fake IDs coming here."

"I accidentally gave my fake ID at the doctor's office."

"Is this a good shirt for my fake ID?"

"Can I use your address for my fake ID? Dad said I couldn't use his."

Applying Yourself

I highly recommend you proofread your kid's applications, especially the essay. Just don't count on your teen being appreciative. One dad told me he used the electronic comment feature to make several suggestions. When he went back in, it said "comment rejected" next to each one. At least he tried.

- My daughter was upset when writing her college essay that she had a healthy home life because it didn't give her enough writing material.
- My daughter asked if she should put "Central American" down on her application. We live in Kentucky.
- My son asked why I was giving him info on Greek life at the colleges he was considering. He thought I was giving him the percentage of Greek people attending.
- My son applied to a Christian college, so he started getting information from other schools. He asked me why he got something from a dental school. It was Oral Roberts University.

Home for the Holidays

If you thought your kid slept a lot during high school, just wait until they come home during college breaks. Their top priorities during their rare waking hours are illustrated below:

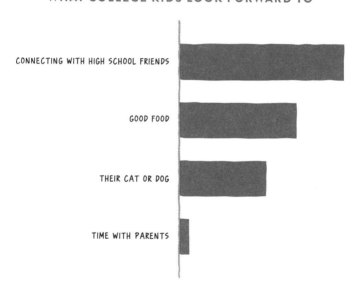

WHAT COLLEGE KIDS LOOK FORWARD TO

CONNECTING WITH HIGH SCHOOL FRIENDS

GOOD FOOD

THEIR CAT OR DOG

TIME WITH PARENTS

Don't be alarmed when your kid sprints past your outstretched arms searching for the cat.

More Questions from College

Think these questions sound basic? At one college orientation, the Dean asked parents to make sure their kids knew the difference between washers and dryers.

After receiving a letter that he had made the Dean's list: "What is this all about?"

"Did I register for selective service? If so, what services did I select?"

"What's the women's version of a fraternity? A maternity?"

"When does the midnight yell at Texas A&M start?"

"What's grandma's actual name?"

"What size jeans do I wear?"

Another of my favorites
is the kid who asked his mom,
"Who's this Dean guy?"

Mailing Stuff

College might be when your kids encounter the postal service for the first time. If you think you don't need to teach them how to mail a letter, think again. I've had professors tell me they spend time on this with students. One of my favorite mail-related stories is about the girl who was applying to renew her passport; because the application required a passport photo, she sent in a photo of her old passport.

"I need some letter sticker things so I can mail something."

"How do I use a mailbox?"

"Do you need envelopes to send postcards?"

"What's postage?"

When asked to send something to his parents: "Our school doesn't have outgoing mail."

"If I put multiple stamps on, do I layer or put them side by side?"

"What is the blue metal box on the sidewalk that I see people putting envelopes into?"

"Will you bring stamps when you come visit. They are so expensive here."

Our 22-year-old asked if we want her to walk in graduation. "Um, yeah, we booked an Airbnb almost a year ago and have 15 relatives coming in, and we've spent a fortune for this moment."

A parent who used to have disposable income

Filling out Forms

Even though it's easier to fill out forms yourself, the entertainment value of seeing college kids do it is worth it. One girl was at the doctor's office, and where the form asked for her street name, she put down her nickname.

A few more *actual* examples:

THE FORM ASKED FOR:	TEENAGER RESPONSE:
PRIMARY CARE PROVIDER	MY MOM
RELATIONSHIP WITH EMERGENCY CONTACT	GOOD
HIGHEST GRADE COMPLETED	A
MARITAL STATUS	BOYFRIEND
ETHNICITY	GEMINI
PLACE OF BIRTH	HOSPITAL
SEX	NOT YET*

*HONORABLE MENTION GOES TO THE KID WHO ANSWERED "ONE TIME IN FLORIDA"

> At the dentist office,
> where the form asked for
> "relationship to patient"
> next to the signature,
> my kid wrote "my dentist."

"What time is noon?"

And More Things Your College-Aged Kids Might Not Know

In addition to the quotes below, you might be surprised how many kids think Lance Armstrong landed on the moon.

"I don't understand keys"

"Is my new niece a boy or girl?"

"Washington DC stands for Da Capital, right?"

"I can use my expired passport to get out of Mexico, can't I?"

"Do bones go in the trash or recycling?"

"Does Super Tuesday have something to do with Lent?"

"Was my job at Taco Bell government or nongovernment?"

"Why did we pick 365 days a year? So random."

"Is autumn fall?"

"Before cell phones, how did you know what time it was?"

"What's the radar thing that tracks Santa? NASDAQ?"

"When does my birth certificate expire?"

"What is my country of citizenship? Quick!"

"Do I put on the bear spray before I go hiking or just if I see a bear?"

"Do islands just float around untethered?"

"How do I get the next sheet off the lint roller?"

"Is my passport good in all 50 states?"

"What's the word for the cages we slept in as babies?"

Things That Might Make You Cry

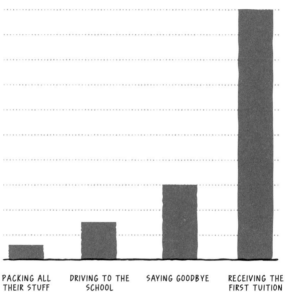

TOUGHEST PARTS ABOUT DROPPING
YOUR KID OFF AT COLLEGE

PACKING ALL THEIR STUFF · DRIVING TO THE SCHOOL · SAYING GOODBYE · RECEIVING THE FIRST TUITION BILL

"Mom, you are
a social liability.
Don't speak."

CHAPTER 7

Teen Language Glossary

IT ANNOYS TEENAGERS when you use words from
their generation. While I don't recommend this, I do
think it's helpful to try to understand what they're
saying. I can't guarantee the accuracy of any of the
following definitions, but it's better than nothing.

WORD	USAGE	DEFINITION
BASIC	THEY WOULDN'T PICK YOU FOR *SURVIVOR*, DAD. YOU'RE TOO OLD AND TOO BASIC.	LAME. UNINSPIRED. OFTEN USED TO REFER TO MY COOKING.
BIRTH GIVER ALTERNATES: BIRTH MOTHER, PROGENITOR, MY SPAWNER, DUDE, AND MOTHER FIGURE	I'M GOING TO NEED YOU TO VENMO ME $30 RN BIRTH MOTHER	MOM
BOUNCE	AFTER THIS COLADA WE NEED TO BOUNCE.	LEAVE. (AS IN YOUR DAUGHTER JUST POLISHED OFF ANOTHER VIRGIN PINA COLADA ON VACATION AND IS READY TO GO.)
BRO ALSO: *BRUH, BRAH*	BRUH, WHEN DOES MY SOCIAL SECURITY NUMBER EXPIRE?	MOTHER. OR FATHER. ALSO, ANY OTHER HUMAN.
CAP	YOU LOOKED 1,000 YEARS OLD WHEN YOU WERE RUNNING FOR THAT AIRPORT SHUTTLE. NO CAP.	CAP ITSELF MEANS BS. SO WHEN USED WITH "NO" IT INDICATES FACT.
CAUGHT LACKING	MY KID CALLS IT CAUGHT LACKING WHEN SPOTTED IN PUBLIC WITH ME.	GETTING CAUGHT DOING SOMETHING YOU DEFINITELY DON'T WANT OTHER PEOPLE SEEING.

WORD	USAGE	DEFINITION
COLONIAL ALSO: MEDIEVAL	WHY ARE WE MAKING OUR OWN PIZZA? WE'RE NOT LIVING IN COLONIAL TIMES.	REFERS TO ANYTHING TEENS PERCEIVE AS BEING OLD FASHIONED (FOR INSTANCE, THE LAST GENERATION IPHONE).
DEAD	BRO I'M DEAD. NO CAP.	FUNNY (AS IN "I'M DYING LAUGHING"). THE NO CAP THING CONFUSES MATTERS THOUGH.
EXTRA	MY HUSBAND SANG A HYMN AT A FUNERAL AND MY SON TOLD HIM TO STOP BEING SO EXTRA.	TOO MUCH. CHILL OUT AND DIAL IT BACK DUDE.
FLEX	WEIRD FLEX, BUT OK (AFTER I MENTIONED THAT I HAD JUST SEEN A HUMMINGBIRD).	SHOWING OFF, LIKE WHEN I INFURIATE MY FAMILY BY USING THE AUTHENTIC PRONUNCIATION OF "CHURRO" IN A MEXICAN RESTAURANT.
GANGSTER	THANKS, GANGSTER.	THIS IS YET ANOTHER WORD FOR MOM.
GATEKEEP	WHY ARE YOU GATEKEEPING THE DORITOS?	TO LIMIT ACCESS, ESPECIALLY TO FOOD YOU WANT TO SAVE FOR YOURSELF.
HITS DIFFERENT	THAT SIP OF WATER AT 3 A.M. JUST HITS DIFFERENT.	WHEN A VERSION OF SOMETHING HAS A DIFFERENT IMPACT. NOW THAT THIS IS THE NAME OF A TAYLOR SWIFT SONG, I SHOULDN'T HAVE TO EXPLAIN IT.

WORD	USAGE	DEFINITION
I JUST ATE THAT	I JUST ATE THAT MIDTERM LIKE GRAHAM CRACKERS AT 12 A.M.	I NAILED IT. C+ AT LEAST.
IT'S GIVING	YOUR BOOTS ARE GIVING COLONIAL SCHOOLBOY. ARE YOU GOING TO START HEEL CLACKING NOW?	TO REMIND OF SOMETHING ELSE. WHEN REFERRING TO A PARENT, IT'S ALWAYS NEGATIVE.
LITERALLY	MY MOUTH IS LITERALLY ON FIRE FROM THESE CHEETOS, BRAH.	WHATEVER THE OPPOSITE OF LITERALLY IS. THIS IS THE MOST COMMONLY USED WORD IN TEENAGER LANGUAGE. LITERALLY.
LOW KEY	ON FATHER'S DAY: "LOW KEY YOU'RE A GOOD DAD'	SORT OF A COMPLIMENT, I'M HOPING.
NOT ME	NOT ME DYING.	ME (CONFUSING, I KNOW)
NOT YOU	NOT YOU GETTING YOUR SANDWICH RIPPED OUT OF YOUR HAND BY THAT SEAGULL.	YOU (OBVIOUSLY). SEEMS TO BE USED TO HIGHLIGHT EMBARRASSING THINGS LIKE MY WEAK HAND STRENGTH.
PILGRIM	DON'T BRING HOMEMADE. WE DON'T NEED TO LOOK LIKE PILGRIMS.	SUGGESTING OLD FASHIONED TIMES — LIKE WHEN YOU WERE GROWING UP IN THE 1630s.
RATCHET	UR POST IS RATCHET. PLEASE DELETE IT.	NOT GOOD. THE DERIVATION OF THIS ONE (AND MOST OTHERS) IS UNCLEAR.

WORD	USAGE	DEFINITION
RIZZ	MOM, WEAR MORE CLOTHES NEXT TIME. NO ONE NEEDS TEENAGE BOYS RIZZIN ON YOU.	CHARISMA USED IN TRYING TO HIT ON SOMEONE. DEFINITELY DON'T TRY TO USE THIS ONE. IT'S CRINGE LEVEL ELEVEN WHEN A PARENT SAYS IT.
SLAP	LUNCH TODAY DID NOT SLAP. NOT YOUR BEST WORK.	"THIS IS GREAT" WHEN USED AS A VERB. AGAIN, PLEASE DON'T TRY TO USE THIS. A MIDDLE-AGED PARENT EXCLAIMING, "THIS SANDWICH SLAPS! THE SOURDOUGH JUST HITS DIFFERENT!" WON'T GO OVER.
TRASH	THE FOOD WE HAVE IS TRASH. I'M NOT BRINGING A BUBLY TO SCHOOL.	BAD. USED AS NOUN, ADVERB, OR ADJECTIVE ("WHY IS YOUR COOKING SO TRASH?").
WEIRD	WHY IS YOUR WINDOW ROLLED DOWN? THAT'S WEIRD.	ANY BEHAVIOR A PARENT DISPLAYS. THIS INCLUDES HOW YOU SMILE, CHEW, SPEAK, ETC. IF YOU'RE HEADING INTO A SOCIAL SITUATION WITH YOUR TEEN, THEY MAY WARN YOU IN ADVANCE, "DON'T BE WEIRD."
ZIP CODING	NOT YOU ZIP CODING ALL FRESHMAN YEAR.	TO DATE MULTIPLE PARTNERS IN DIFFER-ENT GEOGRAPHIES. THE REAL-LIFE VERSION OF "MY GIRLFRIEND LIVES IN CANADA" (ONE OF THEM, ANYWAY).

CHAPTER 8
On Vacation

VACATIONS OFFER THE chance to spend a lot of money and still be criticized by your teenagers. All delayed flights, disappointing meals, and inclement weather will be your fault. And definitely don't act weird by trying to talk to other people in public.

Teens will also find your months of research and planning cringy and annoying. I've been cautioned that if I use the phrase "hidden gem" or "best-kept secret" again, there will be a revolt.

Money is no object to a teenager on vacation with their parents. They're looking for first-class accommodations, separate rooms, etc. When you hear your kid mention they "could go for a steak again," you'll long for the days when they could order off the kid's menu.

Teens will also view the family vacation as a hassle that disrupts their schedule. But it's a classic no-win situation: the one time you try leaving the kids behind, they'll be upset you excluded them. My daughter recently told me she was annoyed that we went to Hawaii without her 2 years before she was born.

do I have to go on the family vacation?

Texted by teenagers around the world when they're
looking to crush their parents' spirits

How to Embarrass Your Kids on Vacation

VACATION EMBARRASSMENT SCALE

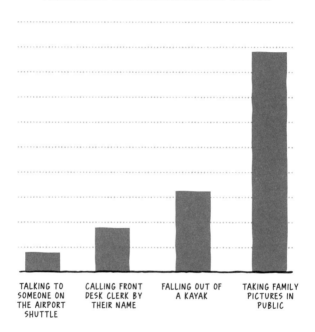

TALKING TO SOMEONE ON THE AIRPORT SHUTTLE

CALLING FRONT DESK CLERK BY THEIR NAME

FALLING OUT OF A KAYAK

TAKING FAMILY PICTURES IN PUBLIC

Speaking foreign languages while traveling also risks embarrassment. Once, in Mexico, I thought the name of our hotel should be pronounced differently in Spanish, so I asked the cab driver to take us to the Marriótt (heavy accent on the last syllable). We arrived at the hotel safely, which is better than the night before, when I misunderstood the bus driver and we boarded a bus traveling away from the beach, headed toward a distant downtown bus depot.

Vacation Mistakes

Try not to injure yourself or be visible in any other way while vacationing with the kids.

- During a family vacation in Montana, I was in a mountain biking accident and was taken to the hospital with a concussion and other injuries. My teenagers were upset that I had "literally ruined a day of vacation."
- I had to apologize for taking a picture of an alligator while on a swamp boat tour in New Orleans.
- While taking a walk on vacation, I had to apologize to my teen girls for having a leaf in my hair.
- My stepdaughter posted pics from our trips with no family in them. Apparently, she travels alone.

Overheard on Vacation

The fact that two of these quotes took place at concerts should deter you from including those in your family vacation.

While at a stadium concert: "Don't stand up when the wave gets around to us."

When her mom clapped after their flight landed: "Mom, nobody does that anymore."

"Next time, can we book the airline seats that recline and they serve you everything?"

"Everyone went to Jamaica. I know like 4 people."

"Don't dance with your arms over your head."

Sharing a Hotel Room

This is one part of vacation that no family member enjoys.

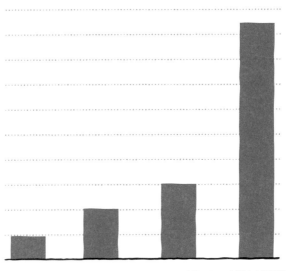

WHAT BOTHERS TEENS ABOUT SHARING A HOTEL ROOM

SLEEPING ON A PULL-OUT SOFA

NO PRIVACY

PARENTS MAKING NOISE IN THE PRE-DAWN HOURS

DAD'S SNORING

If I snore at home, my wife gives me a sharp knee in the back. If I snore on vacation, I can count on multiple children throwing random things in my direction.

Calibrate Your Expectations

WHAT YOU THINK YOU'LL LOSE ON
A FAMILY VACATION

- Stress
- A few pounds
- Your focus on work
- Your attachment to your phone

WHAT YOU'LL ACTUALLY LOSE ON
A FAMILY VACATION

- Patience
- Money
- Energy
- The desire to take another family vacation

Teen:

so we're not doing anything on the 15th right?

Parent:

?? Yes. We are going to Europe.

Top 3 Vacation Activities:
Parents vs. Teens

Unfortunately, there isn't a lot of overlap.

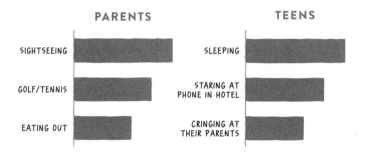

PARENTS	TEENS
SIGHTSEEING	SLEEPING
GOLF/TENNIS	STARING AT PHONE IN HOTEL
EATING OUT	CRINGING AT THEIR PARENTS

A good planning rule of thumb:
for every hour of active time spent
together as a family, allow 4 hours
of time spent isolated from one
another so your teens can recover.

Vacation Activities That Should Be Relaxing but Aren't

Boating

This is a relaxing way to spend the day as long as you don't have to dock, undock, trailer, beach, or anchor the boat. Getting gas, unfurling a rope for tubing, and navigating are also problematic. And if it rains or is partially cloudy, this is a disaster. My kids once accused me of "driving us into the clouds."

Going to the Beach

I guess this can be fun if you enjoy hauling piles of gear from distant parking lots in the blazing sun. Just know your teens will blame you if any of the following occur:

- You stand up and a few grains of sand blow toward them.
- You can't perfectly control the sunscreen mist that wafts in their direction.
- A wind gust turns your umbrella into a dangerous projectile that nearly impales them as it sails down the beach.

Hiking

It's the rare teenager who enjoys hiking. This is especially true if you're on a tropical vacation. Resist the urge to explore some jungle or volcano crater. Near-vertical trails in 90-degree temperatures are not a recipe for success. If you go, don't make the mistake of one dad who didn't bring enough water and insisted on "rationing" it.

Amusement Parks

I remember Disney World as a kid consisting of teacup rides and bumper cars. Today, going to a theme park is more like, "Hey, can we go on the Tower of Death?" On our last trip, the biggest roller coaster I was willing to ride with my then preteen daughter was a Woody Woodpecker–themed child coaster, and I was white-knuckling it the whole time. My wife and son did one of those simulator rides where they shake you back and forth in front of a digital screen. Afterward, we found my wife, who gets motion sickness, sitting on the ground muttering, "I'm going to need a minute here." These places are pretty expensive, but you can get a deal if you go to one in Florida in July.

Pickleball

Just because senior citizens make this look fun and relaxing doesn't mean you should attempt it as a family. There is always one parent who gets hypercompetitive and objects to line calls with John McEnroe's intensity. And at least one kid who couldn't care less and is being "forced" to play. Regardless, the score will be disputed before every point. The game will end when one of the parents either trips and falls or pulls a hamstring, tears their ACL, or ruptures an Achilles.

Back to Reality

TOUGHEST PARTS ABOUT VACATION ENDING

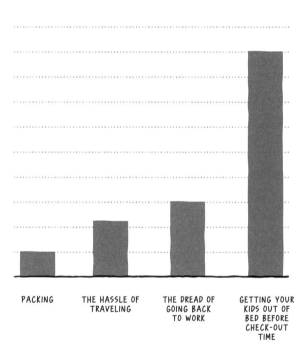

PACKING · THE HASSLE OF TRAVELING · THE DREAD OF GOING BACK TO WORK · GETTING YOUR KIDS OUT OF BED BEFORE CHECK-OUT TIME

CHAPTER 9

Clothes

TEENS AND PARENTS have different senses of style. You'll realize this when they start giving you feedback about your clothing choices. When they ask, "Is that what you wore to work today?," it's not a compliment. Once I picked up my daughter at the airport after she was gone for a week, and her first words to me were, "What kind of shirt is that?" Teens have a long list of items they think we look stupid wearing, but you have to question the credibility of kids who wear hoodies in 95-degree temperatures.

Shopping for clothes with teens can be problematic, too. Some kids enjoy it, while others can't be "hassled" into trying anything on before purchase. The biggest risk, of course, is that you'll encounter someone they know and be seen together. If you run into one of their friends at Target, just remember not to say hi because that's weird.

I once told my daughter she looked really nice. So, then she had to go change.

A mom with zero fashion credibility

"Try again."
And Other Feedback on Parents' Clothing Choices

Having teenagers will either give you a thicker skin or break you. Here are a few responses when seeing their mom or dad dressed and ready to head out the door:

"Nice pants. Didn't feel like matching today?"

"You're literally dressed in rags."

"Your socks are the size of Christmas stockings. They could hang over the fireplace."

Upon seeing their mom in a green coat: "You look just like the hulk."

"You shouldn't wear mini backpack purses."

"You don't wear your AirPods right."

"I don't like having the type of mom who wears glasses."

"You can't leave the house looking like a children's performer."

Pop Quiz: Cold Weather Clothes

What will your kid wear to school in sub-zero temperatures?

A. A warm coat, fully zipped

B. A winter hat

C. Insulated boots

D. Shorts, t-shirt, and crocs

Answer: D. If your kid is super responsible, they might wear an Under Armour hoodie when it snows.

My Kids' Reviews of My Outfits

Once we played a board game that asked everyone to come up with a name if each of us opened a clothing store. "Chip's Tall and Drab" was suggested for mine.

CLOTHING	REVIEW
STRIPED RUGBY SHIRT	LOOKS LIKE SOMETHING A BABY WOULD WEAR.
NEW "DRESS SNEAKERS"	IT'S LIKE YOU'RE TRYING TO LOOK YOUNG WHEN YOU'RE NOT.
NORMAL T-SHIRT	OMG, THAT NECK HOLE IS SO TIGHT. IT LOOKS LIKE IT'S CHOKING YOU. HOW DID YOU EVEN GET THAT OVER YOUR HEAD?
TURQUOISE BLUE SHIRT	BLINDING
BUTTON-DOWN SHIRT WITH WRINKLE-FREE "PERFORMANCE FABRIC"	LOOKS LIKE THE MATERIAL THEY MAKE TENTS FROM
MY CAREFULLY PLANNED OUTFIT BEFORE MY FIRST BIG STAND-UP SHOW	PRETTY BASIC BUT WHATEVER

Body Image Takedowns

Unfortunately, teens can be especially honest when telling you how you look.

- My daughter told me she felt bad for me because my eyelashes are so short.
- My kid asked me to put on makeup before we picked up her friend. I said no. She replied, "I'll just tell her you're sick."
- My teenager said my new haircut makes my head look like an egg.
- My daughter said, "Can you part your hair down the middle before my friends come over?"
- My 15-year-old son said he doesn't like seeing my neck from the side.
- My daughter got mad at me because she inherited my thick, wavy hair and she "can't do anything with it."
- My daughter said my Bitmoji does not have enough wrinkles.

Jeans

WHAT TEENAGE JEANS ARE MADE OF

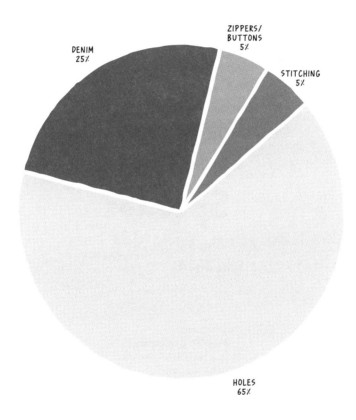

ZIPPERS/
BUTTONS
5%

DENIM
25%

STITCHING
5%

HOLES
65%

Clothes Your Kids Will Mock You for Wearing

I made this word cloud for handy reference. The bigger the word, the more you will be mocked. I asked my kids what other items they might add, but they never responded to my text.

Anything on sale

Reading Glasses

Non-premium brands

Shoes with thick white soles

Mom Jeans

Anything from Costco

Speedos

Crocs   Skechers

Anything your kids wear

Wired Headphones   **Bike Shorts**   New Balance sneakers

Those goofy trainer shoes   Bowling Shoes

Fanny packs

Skinny Jeans

Tight T-shirts

According to my son, some New Balances are popular now but "not the ones parents wear."

Do You Smell That?

HOW POWERFUL ARE THE FOLLOWING TEEN SMELLS?

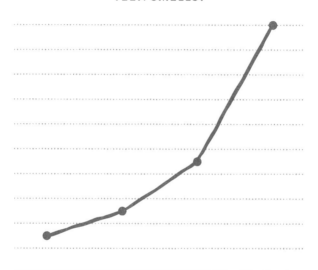

| THEIR SNEAKERS | OLD SOCKS YOU FOUND WEDGED IN THE SOFA | THE HOCKEY EQUIPMENT BAG LEFT IN THE CAR OVERNIGHT | THE ½ CAN OF AXE BODY SPRAY APPLIED BEFORE SCHOOL |

Wardrobe of Embarrassment

If you're seen outside of the house together with your teen, they'll view your clothing choices as a reflection on them.

"Did Dad really wear a beige trench coat to my game?"

"Don't come into the gymnastics studio if you're wearing capri pants."

When being dropped at a friend's house: "I'm sorry about my mom's outfit."

"Don't wear mom jeans to my school again."

"Can you please pick me up? Oh, and make sure you put a bra on."

"Don't wear those generic Beats headphones to the gym. It's embarrassing."

"Have you noticed other moms don't wear sweats?"

Pop Quiz: Shopping

You're back-to-school shopping at Old Navy with your teen-ager and you spot one of their friends. You should:

A. Say hello and ask if they had a good summer
B. Stare straight ahead and pretend you don't see them
C. Dive into the nearest rack of clothes and stay there until the kid has left

Answer: Of course, it's C. If you refuse to make the dive, then your teenager will.

Clothing Experts

Despite their very strong opinions about your wardrobe choices, teens don't actually know everything.

Looking for a sweater: "Where's my yarn shirt?"

"What does khaki mean? Black?"

"Why is there an alligator on my crocs? Random."

At a state park: "Why is that worker dressed like Smokey the Bear mixed with a Girl Scout?"

Getting ready to wash the dishes and looking for the apron: "Where's the robe thing?"

When asked what size shoe he wore: "Medium."

CHAPTER 10

Money

TEENAGERS TYPICALLY DON'T have a lot of their own money, so they're pretty aggressive about spending their parents' funds. One mom asked her daughter to buy some groceries, gave her $60, and when the bill came to $60.41, her daughter asked to be Venmo'd 41 cents.

Most teens lack some basic financial literacy. Bank accounts, checks, taxes, and the like are absolutely mysterious to them (not to mention stamps and envelopes). One mom reported, "After doing poorly his first semester in college, our son said he thought he would just get into investing from his trust fund. He doesn't have one."

Hopefully some of the quotes in this chapter will inspire you to cover the basics before your kids set out on their own.

Happy Mother's Day.
I venmo'd you 6 dollars

Thanks, Bro

ODDS OF YOUR KIDS THANKING YOU WHEN . . .

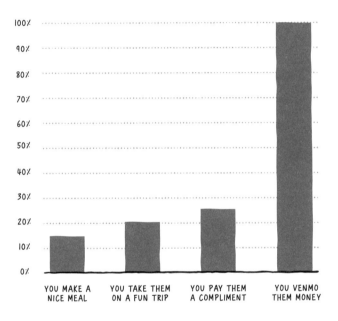

"When should we talk about my inheritance?"

And Other Bold Money Questions

It can't hurt to ask, I guess.

"How do I use your reward points for a hotel?"

After opening a birthday card: "Can't you just put money on a gift card? I hate carrying all this cash."

"Is Halloween considered a legitimate holiday? Like will I get overtime for working it?"

"What's my net worth?"

Pop Quiz: Cash Money

What will your kid do if you give them cash?

A. Drive to the bank and deposit it

B. Spend it immediately at Taco Bell

C. Complain that cash is such a hassle and jam it in a backpack where it will stay for the rest of the school year

D. Take a picture of it with their phone so they can use mobile deposit

Answer Guide:

A. You're raising Warren Buffet, Jr.

B. Hey, at least they're using it.

C. This is the most common behavior, so your kid is average.

D. I wish I were making this one up. Maybe go with a liberal arts college.

"Do I have a brokerage account?"

And More Teenager Money Wisdom

Teens may not know a ton about money, but this doesn't stop some of them from acting as if they do. One kid told his mom he wanted to change his major to finance because he had watched *The Wolf of Wall Street* several times and understood the job. Another mom said that when her son owed her money, he wrote her a check—using her checks. I'm guessing he knew what he was doing. I'm not as sure about the other kids below.

"How do you pay for college anyway? Do they take Venmo?"

"Can I take this parking ticket to a bank teller and pay her or something?"

"What is Wall Street? A journal or something?"

"How did I bounce a check when I still have lots of them left?"

"Do I have a credit score?"

"Annual salary means you get paid that once a year, right?"

"Does McDonald's take cash?"

"Do I just make the check out to 'shoes?'"

"Can we go to the bank and print out some more money?"

"Is American Express a Mastercard?"

On getting their first apartment: "They want first and last month's rent. I didn't even live there last month."

"I don't need toll money. I'll go through the lane on the side where you don't have to pay."

"How late is the ATM open?"

"Is $650K a year enough to live off?"

The Currency of Embarrassment

Try to avoid these payment errors, and keep in mind that 90% of teens think paying in cash "makes us look poor."

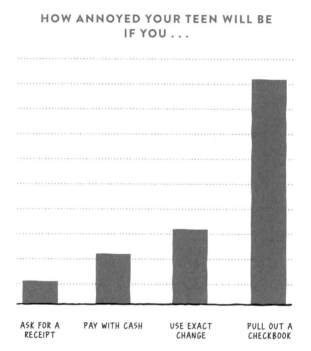

HOW ANNOYED YOUR TEEN WILL BE IF YOU . . .

ASK FOR A RECEIPT · PAY WITH CASH · USE EXACT CHANGE · PULL OUT A CHECKBOOK

Also, if you insert your payment card, you'll be told you should have just tapped it. If you tap it, you'll be told you should have paid with your phone instead.

Insurance

Here's a money-related topic we need to explain better. Need proof? I've heard *multiple* stories of two teens getting into a car accident, exiting their vehicles, and exchanging health insurance information. I've heard of other kids giving auto mechanics their dental insurance. To be fair, some of the terminology can be confusing. I know of one teen who refers to her insurance copay as a cover charge. Honestly, I think that's the clearest description I've heard.

When told her insurance would go up when buying a new car: "Is that a good thing?"

At the ER: "What's our life insurance policy number?"

"The body shop won't take my Cigna card. I thought you told me we had insurance, Mom!"

When the doctor's office asked for her insurance carrier: "State Farm."

"Can my boyfriend use my insurance at the doctor's office?"

"Do I use our health insurance when I take my Guinea pig to the vet?"

"Do I have Medicare?"

"How do I cash in my W2?"

And Other Teen Questions about Taxes

It's best to help your kids fill out their first tax forms. If you don't believe me, look at some of their questions below:

"Are you and dad my dependents?"

"I'm filing jointly, right?"

"Am I a member of the clergy?"

"Am I a ward of the state?"

"How come I have to pay taxes!"

"Have I ever worked for the railroad?"

"What do you use to do taxes, Geico?"

"I thought W2 was a band."

CHAPTER 11

Technology

THIS IS A MINEFIELD, and one area where your teen *actually* knows way more than you do. Mistakes are everywhere to be found. Some are obvious (see my social media guidelines on the next page) and some are subtle. I heard of one kid who stopped following his mom on Instagram because her hashtags were too long. It seems very specific to me, but that was his reason.

Hopefully you paid attention during the communication chapter, because your improper use of technology will only compound those errors.

Social Media Guidelines

Here are my tried-and-true rules for minimizing your teen's outrage.

DO NOT MAKE YOUR INSTAGRAM PUBLIC. I applaud you for even having an Insta account but beware: your kid's friend might stumble on it and realize you exist. If the friend finds it because you tagged your teenager, this is egregiously worse. Even better: stick to Facebook, where no one under 40 will see anything anyway.

DO NOT TAG YOUR KIDS IN SOCIAL MEDIA POSTS: See above. As cute as you think the post is, they will consider it "ratchet" (see my teen language glossary for ratchet definition).

DO NOT COMMENT ON THEIR POSTS: You're obligated to like all their posts, but no comments, please. As one mom was warned, "You are one comment away from being blocked."

DO NOT POST A PICTURE OF YOUR CHILD: You probably think there is an exception for special occasions like birthdays or maybe college graduations, when you're commemorating the expenditure of half your retirement nest egg. But the only exception is if you get preapproval from your kids, which you will not receive.

DO NOT LIKE, FOLLOW, OR COMMENT ON ANY OF YOUR KIDS' FRIENDS' SOCIAL MEDIA ACCOUNTS. This is the worst infraction of all, because in your teen's imagination it will lead to a room full of their classmates pointing at their phones and laughing because you are trying so hard to be cool. My wife was once briefly connected with some of my son's friends on BeReal, and it didn't go well. When it comes to what 18-year-old boys are up to at random times of the day and night, ignorance is better.

As you can see, I couldn't think of any Dos. Any of the above behaviors will risk you being blocked from your kid's account. Want proof?

> "I looked up my son's future college roommate on Facebook and he's now blocked me for 10 years on all social media."

Sometimes you don't even need to do anything to trigger the penalty:

> "My kid preemptively blocked me on TikTok the day I joined."

"Please don't tag me anymore in those posts about loving your kids and crap."

Technology Error Scale

HOW EMBARRASSING ARE YOUR TECHNOLOGY ERRORS?

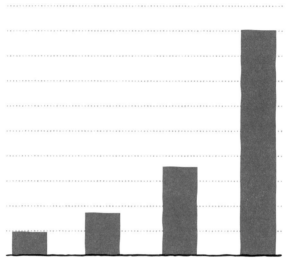

ANSWERING THE PHONE ON SPEAKER

TYPING WITH ONE FINGER

HOLDING THE PHONE TOO CLOSE ON FACETIME

MAKING A SNAPCHAT ACCOUNT

Pop Quiz: Sending Videos

If you see a funny video on social media and send it to your teenager, they will:

A. Watch it right away and thank you for sending it

B. Plan to watch it later, but never do

C. Pretend they watched it and immediately text back a laughing emoji (in less time than it would have taken to play the full video)

D. Delete it immediately because if they click on it, it will mess up their algorithm and they might get served more old people videos

Answer: B, C, and D are all acceptable answers.

Technology Offenses

I didn't respond to a text within 15 seconds

I find this ironic given that it often takes 15 business days for me to get a reply. If a text has to do with a Netflix password, food, asking for money, or needing to get picked up, then it needs to be answered within seconds. I guess that's pretty much all texts. If my daughter sees the 3 dots that indicate I'm typing, she will immediately text back, "Spit it out."

I had too many browser tabs open

I'm not proud of having 99 tabs open, but I'm also not sure why this stresses out my kids. I know it's been 18 months, but I still might make that pasta recipe.

My flashlight was on

The is the new version of driving with your blinker on. It's definitely worse when it happens in public: "At a high school volleyball game, the ref stopped the game and came down his ladder to tell me my flashlight was on."

Quiz: How Annoying Are Your Technology Habits?

Score 1 point for every "yes" answer.

- Has your teen described your phone's font size as comically large?
- Do you have more than 15 browser tabs open on your phone?
- Have you unknowingly turned on your flashlight in the past week?
- Does your phone make a "shutter" sound while taking a picture?
- Does your phone make audible typing sounds?
- Do you have a Facebook account?
- Is your phone's brightness high enough to perform surgery with?
- Is your phone's ringer turned on?
- Do your texts involve punctuation?
- Have you charged your phone when your teen's had a lower battery percent?
- Do you leave voicemails?
- Has your teen criticized the folders your phone screen is organized into?

0 to 2: Impressive. Obviously, you're a teen whose parents have given you this book. I'm surprised you're reading it.

3 to 5: Honestly, pretty good. But if your teen is scoring then you are embarrassing.

6 to 8: OK, Boomer. You know you're draining the battery, right?

9 or more: Low-key cringe. I literally can't with you.

"It's a hashtag, not a pound sign."
And Other Teenager Technology Quotes

"Delete all your social media profiles. My friends found you."

"You accidentally posted a story on Instagram."

"Mom, don't let anyone else know you have an Android. I'll never live it down."

"Delete the marching band post now."

"You need to chill in the family group chat."

"Why are you trying to follow me on Apple Music? That's weird."

"I couldn't finish mowing the grass because my AirPods died halfway through. You wouldn't understand."

"Never snapchat me again."

"do I have to eat dinner with you"

And Other Texts You'll Receive from Your Teenagers Most Frequently

did you transfer the cash yet

I put some stuff in the Amazon cart

Why did you call me

I don't want to go

approve the app

are you going to be near a chipotle today or no

Why You Shouldn't Give Your Kids Your Passwords

At one point my daughter changed my Netflix username to Dope and my avatar to that kid, Will, from *Stranger Things*. This was 4 years ago, so I should probably figure out how to change it back. Every email I get from Netflix starts with "Hi, Dope."

I guess she's not alone, based on the stories I hear from other parents. A few examples:

- My kid changed my phone to autocorrect "you" to "ass." I discovered this after an email to teachers and the principal.
- My teenager changed my Apple username to "Big Chungas," which wasn't a problem until the day I had to go to the Apple store.
- My daughter changed her dad's ringtone to Shania Twain's "Man I Feel Like a Woman." Every time it rang, he was angry.

BONUS: PARENT CONFESSIONS

Because not all the embarrassing things you do fit neatly into the chapters above, here's a quick reminder that there are always more ways to annoy your teens.

- I get reprimanded for getting "too scared" when they scare me.
- I laugh too cheerfully. Sorry about that. I'll be more sullen.
- My teen accused me of counting my money too aggressively at the drive-through.
- Apparently, I'm annoying for tapping my foot to music.
- My eyes blink too loudly.
- My daughter told me I need to smile more at the cashier because I come off like I don't care about them.
- I broke my rib and both kids complained about the noises I made when standing up to reach for something.
- I started singing along to a Weeknd song and my daughter said, "Thanks for ruining the vibe."

I'm engaged lol . . . can't talk my phone is dying

Final Thoughts

PARENTS WITH OLDER KIDS tell me the fun doesn't stop after college. As one mom noted, "My son runs a hedge fund and doesn't know what a cantaloupe is." The crazy texts and questions will keep coming, which I'm looking forward to.

I once read an article about a study that concluded a teenager's use of sarcasm is a sign of intelligence. I guess this means a lot of us are living with geniuses. I'm not sure what definition of intelligence these researchers used, but it obviously didn't include the ability to reseal a box of Cheez-Its.

In all seriousness, I do think humor is a sign of a sharp mind and I believe our kids will use their smarts to create bright futures. At what age this happens might vary. I know of a young woman who only discovered in her mid-20s that groundhogs are real. Before that she thought they were mythical creatures like unicorns. Here's a guide to help determine where your kid is on the continuum.

Readiness Guide for 20-Somethings

What it means if your kid asks these types of questions:

QUESTION	WHAT IT MEANS
"THE LABEL ON THIS IBUPROFEN SAYS I CAN TAKE IT EVERY 4 HOURS—IS THAT TRUE?"	CLOSE ENOUGH. THEY'RE READY TO BE ON THEIR OWN.
"CAN I GET LUNG CANCER FROM SMOKED TURKEY?"	THEY MIGHT NEED A LITTLE MORE TIME.
"WHAT KIND OF ANIMAL IS A SOY?"	UMM . . . HOW BIG IS YOUR BASEMENT?

Acknowledgments

I have to start by thanking so many of you who've shared your funny quotes and stories with me. The online community that's sprung up around *The Leighton Show* has been amazing and humbling. I will always be grateful for your generosity and support.

Thanks to my stellar literary agent, Gillian MacKenzie, for encouraging me on this path and for her excellent guidance and support along the way. Thank you to Ann Treistman at Countryman Press, for believing in this project and for her superb recommendations to make the work stronger. Thanks to Allison Chi for her wonderful design, and thanks to the full team at Countryman for your many contributions.

Thanks to my mom and dad, for setting a great example of how to raise kids in a healthy and loving way. A huge thank you to my wife, Lisa, for humoring me in this weird side hustle, for her kind and supportive feedback, and also for telling me when I'm being dumb.

And, of course, thank you to my two amazing kids, without whom I wouldn't have been inspired to write this book. I know it's tough to get a sense of the real person behind a string of funny text messages, so below is a brief peek behind the curtain.

My daughter is a straight-A student, a highly accomplished classical violin player, competitive swimmer, and, if you encounter her in the real world, she's the kindest and most well-mannered kid you could find. And at home, she roasts me mercilessly. It's like living with Ricky Gervais.

My son is a dean's list student who is now thriving in college. In high school, he was a competitive high jumper and captain of his school's state champion mock trial team. Based on the screaming I regularly hear coming from downstairs, I assume he's also really good at video games. His one main fault is that he's a Celtics fan. Go Sixers.

For the last 7 years, my wife and I have had at least one, and sometimes two, teenagers in the house. It has been the most rewarding experience of our lives.

Finally, I want to acknowledge that not every teen is fortunate enough to grow up in a loving and supportive home. If you want to help make a difference, Preble Street is a wonderful organization that operates several teen services programs, including a shelter for homeless youth (Preblestreet.org).